vibrations of reality

poetry that bridges

oana stefanescu

Soft Altitude Publishing

www.softaltitudepublishing.com

vibrations of reality – poetry that bridges

by Oana Stefanescu

Published by Soft Altitude Publishing

Ottawa, ON, Canada

www.softaltitudepublishing.com

Cover and illustrations by Oana Stefanescu

Author photo by Alex Stefanescu

ISBN 978-1-7387127-2-4

Printed in Canada

First Edition

.

"Oana has done it again. Just like in her first poetry collection, *the stars within us*, her divine inspiration shines through every poem. I was particularly moved by the underlying theme of finding and living one's true purpose, exemplified in poems like "trail", "wide" and "hero". Oana has crafted an inspirational book that everyone should read."

—**Natacha Belair, Award-Winning Author,** *A Stellar Purpose* **trilogy**

I would like to dedicate *vibrations of reality – poetry that bridges* to my husband, Alex. You have been my biggest supporter from the moment we met and you have always helped me make my heart's dreams a reality. I couldn't be more grateful.

In love and immense gratitude,

Oana

about this book

vibrations of reality – poetry that bridges is a collection of poems that bridge the physical world with the non-physical world of imagination, aspirations and dreams. Written from a perspective that lives outside of time, the poems create a synergy between your lived-reality, your spiritual awareness and your soul's highest potential.

Please consider each poem as you would a cup of hot tea, that you might sip slowly, carefully, while focusing on each of your awakening senses as they come into your awareness. The poems are not meant to be read in any specific order; you may enjoy them as you wish.

May this poetry collection help you bridge your worlds and bring you the lightness of clarity as you inch closer to the destiny you are meant to meet.

I wish you all of the abundance, happiness and inner peace possible,

Oana

vibrations of reality

poetry that bridges

the poems

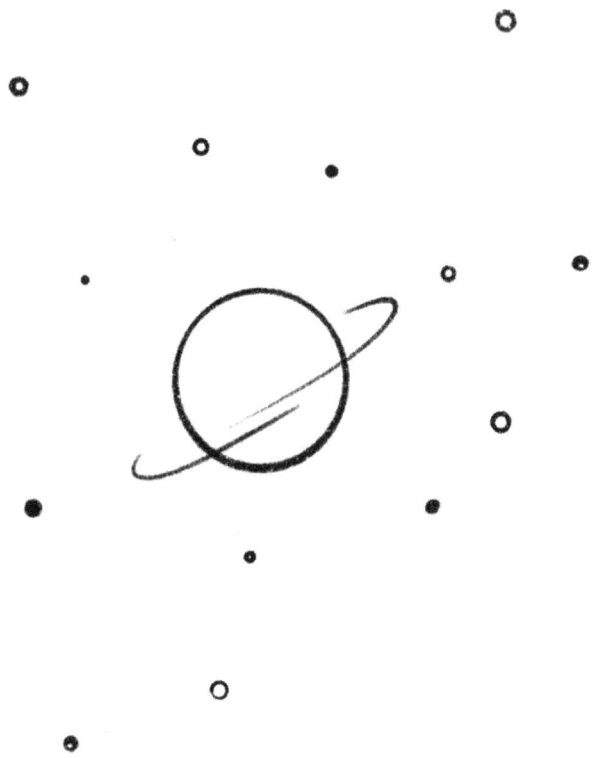

outside of time

I come from

a place

outside of time

and I remember

from before

I remember

the lightness

floating

the colours

I come from

a place

outside of time

and I remember

the feeling

of eternity

of unity

and freedom

beyond comprehension

I come from

a place

outside of time

where we can

simply be

we are

expansion

and possibility

itself

human structures

don't apply

in that space

outside of time

let's remember

together

that space

it's where
we all come from
that place
outside of time

we are the power
of creation
and we truly can
remember

we are
at the beginning
and we become
the beginning
itself
when we reach
into that space
outside of time

floating

float at ease
and understand
the power of thought
you have at hand

bring it forth
and use it wise
the energy
as it starts to rise

float at ease
and float to see
the wonderful you
you are going to be

the higher path

there are as many paths to take

as there are intersections

in crochets

and weaves inside of rugs

but one path rises

as the sun

above the horizon

of waves in thought

and actions in plan

the higher path

is the one that calls

out

to you

with fragile voice

at first

which then begins to

boom

as your heartbeats

quicken

and wit increases

with every

smile

that unfolds upon you

as you learn to know

and know to learn

your truth

your light

your heart

and how to follow

the often quite

painterly

messages they send you

the higher path is

the only path

that will take you

back to

none other

than

your truth

your heart

your destiny

finally

connecting

the bridge

between

you

and

your soul

frame of mind

stretch that canvas

lay down your thoughts

in your own frame of mind

in your colours of choice

build up the shapes and forms

with palette knives and

brushes filled with memories

that swiftly come and go

leaving traces, emotions

colours and movements

turn to the window

and bravely show the world

your frame of mind

what you see

there's a big difference
between
what you see and what really is

what is coming
right
around the corner
just ready to please

you often worry too much
because you do not see
the opportunities that are
so close in breaking to be

snapping open the
constrictions you held
onto
so tightly
in case they help

but the potential

sits in waiting

patiently

in the vibrations

of what you feel

and in the

vibrations

of the opportunities

about to show up

at your door

weaving

I know not much

about weaving

except

when stories do

as they move in and out

of themselves

and the narrative that holds

them true

I know not much

about weaving

except

for feelings

as they do

shifting

and

morphing

in and out of each other

until it becomes

a little hard

to tell what's true

I know not much
about weaving
except
when our thoughts
cannot stop
to circle and nosedive
from the known
to the unfamiliar
where everything
may just
become true

painting

I like to paint with words

not because I'm out of acrylics

but because words

hold much more meaning

than the texture of some paint

human-made

words carry with them

an ancient history

as spoken

as thought

as written

as read

in lifetimes

                      tied

             with a thread

in the records

akashic or otherwise

of each and every soul

words contain

a lifetime of energy

used and misused

so carefully over time

that they are now ripe

of things

we cannot find

with eyes

or in mind

they're felt only in our souls

painting with words

invokes the unseen

and the unfelt

that is and

that has been

right along with what

may be

brought forth
by consideration

we did it

you and me
we exchanged
and we painted
with words

we forged our path
           together

we painted

together

signs come in

from outside your world

sometimes

as if a thought unspoken

right from your own self

like the magnet

you once found

at the bus stop

on the ground

it read "together"

it lives on your fridge door

after ten years or more

since you found it

and you're still

magnetically

and lovingly

together

both worlds

it's not enough

to live above it all

but neither is it enough

to live attached

to the hardness

the dense and visible

reality

of this world

a life fully experienced

is one that lives

in both worlds

all at once

one foot in each

and heart in the middle

open to the frequency

of the true path

of your soul

lean in

tune into the waves

of higher consciousness

while living

loving and experiencing

what your reality

puts before you

day to day

face to face

touch to feel

and heart to see

both of your worlds

come together

as one

lend a hand

reach out

from your soul to theirs

and lend a hand

in times of need

without expectation

without confetti

without the eyes

of one or many

lend a hand

and open your heart

we're ready to heal

what has been

tearing us apart

maybe it's not

a hand they need

but maybe an ear

or maybe

they just

need to feel

that

    someone

is near

lend a hand

in ways unseen

just hold the other

in love

in happiness

here

in this beautiful dream

your energy

when you walk into a room
the aura you exude
rushes through the space
like a wave of light
unseen
but deeply felt
by anyone
more attuned
to textures of the soul

you influence the world around
you do it in the dark
without the slightest sound

by simply being
by being exactly
who you are

you move the world
as you move your thoughts

and what surrounds

you are a force

you make what you are
and create what can be
keep strong
and keep on going

you might just
create and manifest
a whole new kind of story

you are

have you ever felt
that something big
pushed by powers unseen
is meant to
take you by surprise?

an explosion of awareness
a shift in the matrix
a life-changing tumble
as new energies unfold?

it is all here
and it is right now

that power is you
and within you
it's the path
you are already on

all this time

you have waited

you have been waiting

for you

the power

the event

the movement

the shift

all of it is

sparked by the light

inside of

you

narratives of time

lying inside
the delineation
of time
just on the edges
of narratives playing out
writing themselves
out of thin air

as you move along
through the days
and the nights
that mark our time
you sometimes forget
to look to the edges
and notice if
the undulations of time
are to your liking

you are the writer
creating the space

in time

as we walk through it

together

happy, sad, or neutral

we move along

and as we glide

do not forget to remember

that it is you

you are the narrator

of the narratives of time

with the tide

the sadness

        inside

is a side effect of the

        ride

it won't serve to

        hide

just take it in

        stride

let the feelings

        glide

as they come

        up

        with the

        tide

the lightness within

the lightness within

permeates

your boundaries

makes soft

the solidity

of your being

and disperses

into the openness

of reception

waiting in readiness

for something

to change

to grow

to morph

to be

to show

in natural authenticity

in natural beauty

from the lightness within

the light in your eyes

the light in your eyes
speaks to me
with words unheard

behold me gently
across the room
cradling my heart

for one second
at a time
as you walk

towards me
to wrap
your hand in mine
and to share

the unmistakable light
in your eyes
with mine

waves of light

in this world that seems so tight
with boxes and checkmarks
you keep having to fight
you will find your freedom
if you follow your light

shine brightly
and illuminate your path
do it your own way
in your choice
of language and math

make a choice
then make the change
moving on
from times of rage

in this world that seems so tight
make it soft with waves of light

surrender

surrender to the flow
seeping underneath your door
to the gust and flurry
from the underside
to the push and pull
from the other-side

open your door
and feel the pressure on your face
as it moves curtains made of lace
and step into the unknown

surrendering to the flow
feeling the movement
giving space to the unseen

you are about to move
quite far
from where
you have already been

the wind

the wind will take you
up and away
from the feelings of stillness
and the knowing
you have known everyday

allow the movement
to sweep through your soul
allow it to shift
your post and your goal

the wind has a plan
unbeknownst to us all
following a map
and a destiny call

you have opened the door
now you are starting to sway
teetering between potentials
and lifetimes, right here, today

my dream-come-true

I make my decision
clearly and right now
define my dream
choose to do it
and make a vow
because I know
in many ways
my dream already
is

it is here, alive
and blossoming
with
the buds
of so many hopes

these dreams
that I hold onto
as tightly as
an anchored rope

I'm steady

and aware

even as the nail

may have flown

or the cord unravelled

on its own

my intention

is deeply sown

I take a step toward

with thoughts sharp

as swords

in a suit of air

based on words

decisive, confident

as permanent

as change

with a careful plan

I shift and morph

to become

the butterfly

I really am

I embody my truth

I hold my heart close

I live what I love

and I love what I chose

whispers

the chirping of birds
and dancing leaves in the trees
are whispers of love
from the heart
of our existence

we are the shadows of roots
that grow from the ground
though mobile and free
like the wind in the trees

we are the whispers of the earth
we are free to choose and see
how to whisper more beautifully
with compassionate intention
and from a higher vibration

we are the whispers
that all the world can see

heart over mind

choosing heart over mind

refusing to hide

the true nature of my being

no longer deceiving

neither you nor myself

I'm ready to take

my old book off the shelf

time to pack away

the readings

the diagrams

and also

the paper they're on

and the pen I used too

they're the old story

that's long and far gone

from a world that shaped me

in ways that previously won

the thoughts and the customs
the looks and the feels
of an old world
with broken wheels

I'm here to create
and create and create
myself, my life
and the new world to come
with new value
and added weight

I turn to my heart
for the purest vibration
the truest guide of all
I choose heart over mind

the power always glows
from deep inside

channelling wisdom

and the most loving intention

it's my lamppost in the dark

as I move into my heart

and navigate

into the depths of creation

your dream

dream your dream
and dream it loud
with a stick
or in a cloud

write it down
and give it voice
making it real
is always your choice

you have the power
since now you've seen
what your heart has held onto
was always your dream

feel the energy

when I'm still
I can feel
the unseen
as if from behind
a screen
energies flowing around
like swarms of insects
without a single sound

my body is clear
and my awareness is acute
I breathe intentionally
as I ground
and I deeply root

I quietly notice
some changes around me
and movements inside

like wafts of air

or bubbles of sound

ribbons may be pulling

yet I am firmly on the ground

I am still

I can feel my way

which actions to take

which directions to turn

what to create

which seeds to sow

and how to grow

I am guided

and protected

when I am still

I feel the energy

smile

spread kindness

as you move from place

to

    place

soften your gaze

and soften

your

    face

to greet another

with the warmth of

your

    being-ness

a soft face in

a shared place

can

    unstick

the tapes that keep

us from sliding

into

    oneness

we shift back into unity

through the exchange of

one

    smile

smile to myself

when no one is near
and I need a hand
I hold myself

I walked through the sun
got wet in the rain
and I love who I've become
after the smiles and the pain

I've grown so much
not from, but to
who I was
before
before all the lights
and the fully scripted show

the burdens, the heartbreaks
the dreams and the wins
there are more to come –
more of everything

I smile to myself

in gratitude

because I know I will do well

because I worked so hard

and came out of my shell

I smile to myself

so I can undoubtedly know

that I love me so much

and that I will never let me go

say yes

the flow won't be

if there is no room

and too much

lies

in your way

or at your feet

I say yes

yes to more

room to breathe

space to move

a silly dance

a funny face

yes to what my heart

wants

my body to feel

in that moment

and room is made

stale furniture cleared

now there's some space

on the rug

to spin and dance

with eyes closed

smile spreading

and heart

open once more

I can spin

and finally let go

when I say

yes

silent mind

one day I listened
and I noticed
that there was nothing
left to hear
in my mind's hidden ear

all the inner work
the meditation
the witnessing
of thought, memory
and fear

finally
I am in the quiet
of my mind

I must have watched
my thoughts so closely
that they became shy
at being observed

they like yapping

but when I stopped

and really listened

they ran out of things to say

that made space

which I now carry

in my heart

every day

now I feel a peace

I never knew

I could feel

my silent mind

allowed it

and made it real

inner breeze

when my thoughts went silent
a breeze began to blow

I became a cave
steady, sturdy
hollow
yet not

I became so much more aware
of my edges, my roundness
of being
my sturdy shell
melting
into one
with the earth and the water
and the tides flowing
over my edge
and into my belly

I hold the treasures

of the sand

of the earth

of the stars

and their mysteries

flowing in and out

of my heart and my soul

on the shoulders of the breeze

I am steady

sturdier

more aware

more alive

the inner breeze flows

my lightness and darkness

in perfect rhythm

as I exist

by the sea

of my life

antenna

the new energy of the earth

brings you into

a state of awareness

that might at first be shocking

suddenly you feel more

sensations

emotions

feelings

all

more acute

you are not alone

you are tuning up

to tune in better

to the healing

to the mysteries

to the knowledge

coming up

in your awareness

as your consciousness

levels up and up

you become more

an antenna

as your sensitivity brings

thoughts and images

as you pick up the signal

of your higher self

tune in

to the oneness

of all

stranger's gaze

I'm thinking of a moment
I most recently felt fear

and I sat with it
like with a friend over coffee
except it wasn't a friend
at all

I was ready to be scolded
having done this or that
you know, the
w r o n g   w a y
… again

to my surprise
as I sat with it
I had my coffee in peace
because
it had nothing to say
it just sat there

its stare uncomfortable

yet

… nothing

that's when I realised

I was sitting with

a complete stranger

it was as startled as I was

we both waited

… to see

how would I react?

what would I do?

well, I finished my coffee

as I was there to do

we begin

the world turns

time passes

and we begin

new feelings are birthed

into our bodies

and into the experience

as we begin

to be new beings

stepping over

the threshold

of the old

wooden doorway

a portal between rooms

a new room

a new life

a new way of being

as the world turns

as time passes

we begin

the compass

the world turns indeed
as does the compass

the tool we used
that we relied on
that we knew

suddenly the compass
finds more than one north

and it twists and turns

trying
and trying
to find its way
as it used to be told

the old way is out
of touch
yet still in sight

while

the new way is in

our reach

but not yet in our sight

while

the compass remains

our tool of choice

and we watch

unknowing

of the way

or of where

we even want to go

as the compass turns,

where

do *you* want to go?

you begin

with your compass
or without
are you ready?

maybe you know
or maybe not yet
what you are about

to make
what you are about
to get

one step at first
and then
a few more

your destiny lies
along the shore

of the dreams

your heart has drawn

within your being

within your mind

with the beauty of a swan

in thought as you create

let go

lean in

glide onto your path

dive into

your dream

take the idea for a spin

your heart will

lead from within

that's where

you begin

the swan

glide elegantly
like a swan
on the waters
of your inner peace

the water is
yours

your feathers are ready

your eyes glistening
with faith

and the goodness
about to materialize
right before
your very eyes

the universe

is ready

and waiting

for you to become

the swan

ready?

are you ready

for what

you've never expected?

the world turns

the water flows

destinies converge

now

a new ship

has arrived

and it is

      coming

          ashore

are you ready

to step

aboard?

swim

swim in the rain

as it washes away

the dust

the cobwebs

and the lost tears

that fall through

the cracks

appearing over time

swim through

and float about

nothing can stop you

from gliding around

and building your dream

now outstretch your arms

and set the scene

purple

shrouded in purple

different

and differently wrapped

than the time

that has snapped

the line

so finely marinated

in the brine

of certain choices

and thoughts

seen

as through

glasses of wine

shrouded in purple

glimmers

look carefully

feel in and then you'll see

the glimmers

the stars

the flashes

of a parallel life

in a parallel place

lived by a different you

with a different face

each life is a path

with a series of choices

varied perspectives

spoken and retold

in unrecognized voices

the glimmers bring you back

to where you belong

to the present moment

and to your precious song

aboard

you took a breath
and also took
your heart in both hands

with nothing else
but your memories intact
without knowing
a single fact

you did it
you took a plunge
a risk and a lunge
but upwards in the air
with flow
even under the stare
of that stranger

that keeps looking
through your shoulder
following

your every move

even under the gaze

untrusting and unsure

of what you can possibly do more

trust

check the planks

plant your dreams

and grow the plants

while you're

aboard

timelines

imagine

destiny jumping

as if taking a new street

attached to the last

yet veering

in a whole new direction

with wit

and

disorientation

opening onto

another presentation

of the life that can be

yours

here

right next to me

or

right by

your own higher self

that you feel

next to you

but cannot see

things are not linear

so allow and feel

without any fear

dreams that are

the dreams you have

stand tall

beneath your feet

like towers

sturdy

looking into the distance

from the sunrise

of your soul

the dreams you have

are

dreams that are

they're

towers

already built

just wait

for the fog to lift

as will your spirit

when you see

that all of your dreams

are dreams that are

sunshine in my hand

I hold
sunshine in my hand
I brought it here
just for you
to show you my love
and my entire truth

the sunshine in my hand
has the light
to heal the wounds

from the shattered hearts
and splintered dreams
left behind
the lifetimes of mankind

I hold so much
sunshine in my hand
I brought it here
just for you

to show you your love

and your entire truth

beneath

beneath the folds
you hide behind
like layers in a dream

cozy layers of fantasy
and downy
of impermeable heat

bundled up against
the sting of unrequited dreams
and blizzards

blowing snowy thoughts
chiselled in between
story mountains from old dreams

beneath the folds
of fleece and fur
a thin barrier to frost

your true nature awaits

another breath again

a warm belly undulates

filled so softly

with a fate

about to unroll

as spring

uncovers

all

in your shoes

slipping in and out

of shoes

slippers or boots

that you wear

as you wear your self

walk into your day

saying "hi" along the way

to fellow passengers

of life

who

slip into theirs

as you step towards

your truth

magician's hat

the curtains are clear

can you peel them back?

touch them carefully

and hold steady

your magician's hat

you see worlds beyond

worlds within

worlds to the side

and everywhere between

raise your vibration

if you don't have a wand

smile from your heart

and tip your magician's hat

like a suit

life is like a suit

you wear

to keep your soul

wrapped

if only

for a moment

in the experience

of a day

slip into your shoes

and slip into your life

knowing

it is a gift to be here

to follow your path

carried gently

by your soul

and the soles

of your shoes

add on a blazer

of importance

for your next pursuit

love

today

take in some sun

enjoy it with fruit

wear everything carefully

and preciously

like a sunday suit

trail

right beneath your feet
there is a trail you cannot see

to take you fast or move you slow
you'll always get to where
you have been destined to go

that path you cannot see
pulls you like a string
magnetically

this trail of yours was mapped by you
before you came down to earth

you came here to do great things
there's something
you must birth
and your trail
will take you there
if you follow with great care

the planned path

of the snail

will take you -

just keep your eyes on the trail

my tree

I have a tree

it was planted in my name

I was excited to see it grow

I couldn't see it after all

I was moved away

but grow it sure did

all on its own

not a complaint to say

I have a tree

it blooms in spring

with magic petals

of white and raspberry

a magnolia dream rhapsody

the petals cover the sidewalk

when they float towards the ground

they leave a soft mess

and perfumed air all around

I know it is there

outside my childhood home

rooting my name and wishes

into the ground below

holding space for my history

from a short lifetime ago

meet your tree

where does your tree stand?
who planted it for you?

what will you do
when you come
face to face

with the trunk
holding and growing
your roots?

will you be thankful
will you feel at peace

will you be ready
will you put your heart
at ease?

what was your beginning?

you needed one to be

here in this moment
looking at your tree

wide

life can be better
it can be as you wish

it begins with a belief
and constant sighs of relief

the universe holds you
you are its child after all

and the energies support you
picking you up fall after fall

life can be better
set your intentions free

ask for what you'd like
to do, have, or be

the universe holds you
and when you finally decide

to hold yourself in love

your true path will open wide

in your mind

manifest inside your mind
the life you
wish to live

the twists and turns of this new ride
will fill you with questions and answers
and it will spin you
until you give

your heart and soul what you deserve
the old ways you
must outlive
off the common path you must swerve

instead build your very own road
and your old mistakes
forgive

get ready to plan inside your mind
new ways of doing

of being and seeing

consult your heart as well and find

every move is for your growth

and for your spiritual wellbeing

make it yourself

the world will not present you
with the life that you dream
you have to go forward
you have to make it be

for dreams to be
you must do things anew
leave behind the tried
and what you thought was true

dive into the discomfort
the blurry vision and the fog
prepare to run a marathon
of wit and of resilience
and with quiet dedication

keep notes inside your log
leaving clues for those who follow
since you may now be the first

diving into the unknown

with a deep and unquenched thirst

first

there must always be

someone

to go

first

in order

to start something new

to bring to the world

what we may have believed

couldn't come true

right now

in this moment

is that person

you?

hero

you have stepped in
to this life
to change the world

the world
as you know it
is going to shift
as souls like you
repair the rift

and transform the earth
into what she was meant to be
let her flourish, in love

my hero, wish and dream
make it be

stand strong

stand strong in your belief
that you're here
to make a shift
you have a purpose
you have a plan
and you will change
the very rules of the game

stand strong in your heart
it will guide you
on your way
to the happiness you deserve
in your life
throughout your stay

stand strong in your courage
you have what it takes

to be the you
you came here to be

and to shine brightly

now

lead the way

steps

slip under your blanket
warm up with some tea
get ready to write
get ready to be

whisked away to
your land of dreams
from the night, from the day
or from lifetimes far away

dream from your heart
and consider your soul
they are your guiding family
and they know you
as a whole

write down your dreams
and think of some steps
decide in the here and now
you'll forget your regrets

now begin climbing

the hills and mountains

that you wrote and created

and with every step

rise

higher within yourself

and begin to feast your eyes

on the incredible scene

of your inner sun

rise

sunrise

the sun rises

in the east

but it rises inside you as well

it rises when you realize

what is you

and what is shell

you are made of stars

you are made of suns

your soul is a well

of energy that glides

pulling the veil

of understanding

over the earth

and wrapped

within the tides

between lay lines

and growing vines

illuminate your heart

illuminate your eyes

as you witness

the unfolding

of your own

sunrise

direct your thoughts

follow the path
your thoughts choose to take
observe from a distance
before you partake

when you hear them
chattering among themselves
what is of interest to
those busy little elves?

listening from a distance
would you say you agree
with the words that you hear
and the movements you can see?

watch them today

see how you feel
then come back again
as if to a reel

are your thoughts useful

are they helpful, are they kind?

are your thoughts supportive

or do they keep you blind?

from your own beauty

from your own power

do they keep distracting you

minute after minute

and hour after hour?

now that you have witnessed

your own thoughts with open eyes

you know their truth

without their disguise

this new perspective

makes you a better guide

it's time to gather and reconcile

your little elves inside

direct them gently, with love
teach them how to meditate
and how they can support you
in a way they can relate

sparkle

sparkle and shine
my glorious friend
sparkle and shine
with greater dreams yet

your heart is built
for wishing
for guiding
and for light
brighter than a bulb
as it shines with insight

follow your own sparkle
and please spread your shine
illuminate the path
for your new world and mine

understanding

I open my mind

and allow what may come

so aware

of how I am and how I'm not

the only one

a new understanding

of who I am

of who I be

and of the world that will

you see

I am ready for it all

fresh sunshine expanding

along the horizon unfolds

an ocean of understanding

miracles

you are built
to do incredible things

you were meant
to be here
in this life
right now

the power
of your thoughts
your heart
and your soul
is something that
no one other than you
can control

plan your ship
build it
and sail it too
take it to seas

completely

unknown

to you

sail on the water

on land

and in the sky

if you're driven to do it

place no importance

on the "why"

you are built for miracles

just watch

as you make them be

one by one

you will

starting this year

grow into

"you"

and then
you will make
all your miracles
into physical
realities too

vibrations of reality

the vibrations of reality
can almost never be seen

they pull you instead
as they leave a thread

loose and hanging

dangling gently

between
            dimensions

of light, shadows
and of understanding

feel them within
they move the core
of your very being

a whisper

with a touch

only you can feel

and know

those stories and concertos

from times long ago

between

life and your dreams

walking

     running

         or in flight

allow yourself

to feel more

more visions and sensations

more than ever before

the closer you get

to the heart

of what counts

the higher you rise

to meet

the signals

and the shocks

begin riding the waves

of the future

slowly embody

the vibrations and the path

shaking you

out of the old

and into the new

into the lightness

of frequency

as you create

and then embrace

as you rise

and as you flow with

the new vibrations

of

   reality

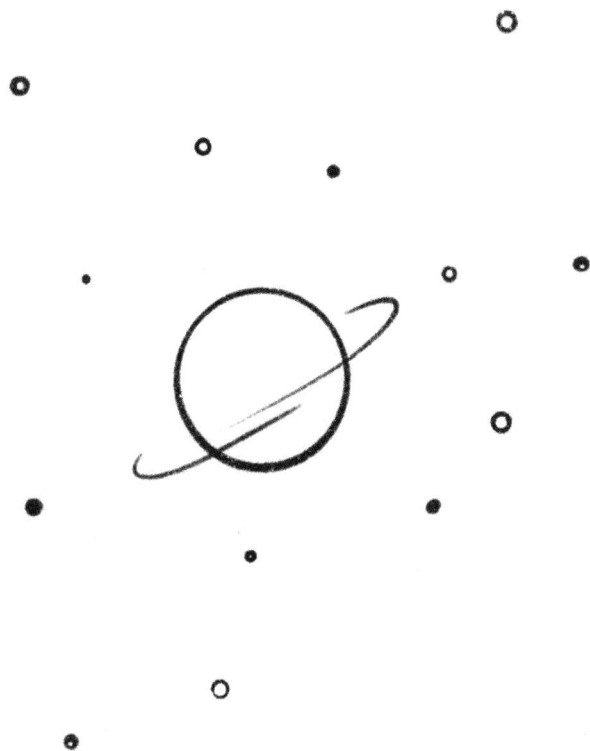

thank you

Dear reader,

I hope that my poems warmed your heart, soothed your soul and inspired you to bridge your reality and your dreams.

May you forever live your heart's hopes, wishes and dreams,

Oana

acknowledgements

Before the cover closes, I wish to offer a few words of gratitude, as I send my second poetry collection out from my heart directly to yours.

First, I would like to thank my husband, Alex. Thank you so much for your continued support and encouragement as I venture to reach for my dreams, one by one.

I would like to thank each member of my family; you have been my biggest fans. Thank you so much for believing in me!

A big thank you to Natacha Belair, award-winning author of the *A Stellar Purpose* trilogy, for your support and for your kind words to my readers!

To my readers, I am humbled by your support for and appreciation of my first book, *the stars within us – high frequency spiritual poetry*. I am deeply moved by your wonderful feedback and reviews and I hope that *vibrations of reality – poetry that bridges* will also find a special place in your heart.

In love and gratitude,

Oana

PS. Please share this book with someone you love!

about the author

My name is Oana Stefanescu and I am the author of *vibrations of reality – poetry that bridges* (2024) and *the stars within us – high frequency spiritual poetry* (2022).

I am a mom of two, an educator, an artist and a Reiki Master. Having had strong intuitive abilities and a deep connection with the spirit realm since childhood, I have been learning about and exploring metaphysical topics ever since. I apply my intuition, spiritual knowledge and energy healing to everything I create, including my writing, my artwork and my teaching. At every opportunity, I wish to uplift and inspire my readers and my students and to bring awareness to their own inner strength, joy and highest potential.

As an educator and a visual artist, I also followed my life-long dream and launched

Soft Altitude Arts, my own art school, in Ottawa, Canada.

I graduated from the University of Ottawa with degrees in English Literature, in Art History and Theory and in Education.

I was born in Romania and I currently live in Canada with my family.

For more information about me or my upcoming books, projects and events, please visit my personal website at www.oanas.ca.

Oana Stefanescu

Soft Altitude Publishing

www.softaltitudepublishing.com